PRAISE FOR RESTORED

"Lisa has a beautiful way of challenging and encouraging you in your walk with the Lord and following Him through her writing. Through personal stories and Scripture, she gives practical insight and helpful tools to grow as a person and a follower of Christ. She truly has a way of connecting with the reader!"

  —ALESHA CULVER LIMBO

"In *Restored: A Journey from Ordinary to Extraordinary*, Lisa shares her vulnerabilities and her encounters with the Lord in a way that draws the reader into a relationship with her and, ultimately, with Jesus. Her writing flows like an intimate conversation over coffee with a friend. A friend who serves as a trusted mentor has walked this path and, through Scripture and her own life experiences, sheds light on our path to an extraordinary life of purpose and love."

  —AMY JULIAN, Director of Evangelization

"I first met Lisa on Zoom to discuss a book I wanted her to publish. Within a few minutes of sitting with her, I could feel a profound 'softness' about her. The feeling was close to bringing me to tears as I could feel her connection to God. In this book, Lisa is bringing her awareness of our call as Sisters to hold hands with one another. To rise and do the extraordinary work God is asking us to do. This is a privilege to work for God — let's hold hands and become God's version of extraordinary. I am in!"

  —GAIL WEST, Gail West Studio,
  Prophetic Artist, Author

"As Lisa draws the reader deeper into their spiritual life through this book, we come to understand where our life has been, where we are now, and how our life can be "extraordinary." The book is easy to understand, and through Scripture and reflection questions, we begin to look into our hearts to see the choices we can make every day to have an extraordinary life. These choices will allow us to "Be who God meant us to be and set the world on fire." (St. Catherine of Siena). I am looking forward to discussing this book with my Bible Study."

  —JANE BARZ
  Council for Pentecost Today USA

"*Restored: A Journey from Ordinary to Extraordinary* challenges one right out of the gate. The Holy Spirit moves from sentence to sentence, moving one's heart and mind from desperation to hopefulness and confidence that God is moving in our lives in extraordinary ways. Lisa uses Scripture and personal witness that readers can identify with, step into, and grow! Definitely a must-read!"

—MAVIS KEMNITZ

"Lisa Fahey invites us into relatable, real, and raw portions of her life to serve as arrows that lead the reader into greater depth and awareness. Lisa is a 'we will do this together' kind of writer, and she masterfully lets us know that we are not alone and can do this together. Lisa's writing also incorporates questions that probe into personal clarity for their authentic self to transform into the extraordinary. Her use of Scripture envelopes the reader like a warm blanket on a cold day as the verses provide comfort and hope of His promises for the more in our lives."

—MICHELLE MAY, CEO G.A.T.E Consulting LLC, Executive
Director of Black Hills Christian Women's Conference

"Lisa's unique gift of translating Scripture into real-life applications is apparent in her work. She authentically and vulnerably shares her personal experiences with the Lord, inviting her readers to come along and learn from her journey. Her writings express an open invitation for readers to relate and draw insight from their lives."

—PASTOR JULIE NORWOOD, CEO
& Founder Big Truth Ministries

"Lisa's writings encourage ordinary people to do extra-ordinary things through a relationship with Jesus. Extraordinary things aren't necessarily what you might envision. They are the extra "ordinary" things done out of obedience to those around you. Lisa shares personal experiences and practical ways to encourage her readers to hear the voice of God in their own lives. As a personal friend of Lisa's, I have witnessed the multiple ways Lisa has obediently enacted the nudges from the Lord to sit with, encourage, and help those whom God has placed on her heart."

—TYLEE PETERSON

"In Lisa's newest book, she compels her readers to seek after the life they've always dreamed of, a life in partnership with the Holy Spirit, guided by God's promises to give us more than all we could ever hope for or imagine. Why not reach for an extraordinary life which God has prepared for us? Lisa shares her own real-life experiences, alongside practical steps to achieve a closer walk with Jesus, knowing that God desires only what's best for us, and wants us to live every day as an EXTRAordinary day with Him. Lisa has gained my deepest respect through the years under her leadership and teaching, always bringing it back to the Gospel."

—VICKI FURNISH

RESTORED

A DISCERNMENT COMPANION JOURNAL

A JOURNEY FROM
ORDINARY TO EXTRAORDINARY

Lisa Fahey

ISBN: 979-8-9881344-1-1

Design by Heidi Caperton

Printed in the United States of America.

INTRODUCTION

How often have you read a book with exercises or questions after each chapter and thought, "Oh, I should get a pen and paper and do what the author suggests or answer the questions?" I am guilty of not recording my answers to the questions or exercises because I have everything sorted out in my head and feel it will be just as effective. I don't know about you, but I often have trouble recalling what I had for lunch, much less how I answered the questions. Therefore, the *Restored Discernment Companion Journal* could be helpful as you read along to help you discover why you're stuck and how to break through.

As you read through each chapter, you may find an exercise I suggest to gain clarity. Space is provided in the journal for you to write and hash things out. The questions at the end of each chapter of *Restored* can also be found in this journal so that you can write down your responses. After each chapter, I've included a Discerning God's Voice exercise for you to read over and record any keywords or concepts that come to mind as you read God's Word. Reading God's Word may give you the perspective and clarity you need to break through in places where you feel trapped. I am confident that the Discerning God's Voice exercise will be super helpful.

Although I recognize that using the *Restored Discernment Companion Journal* will be an extra step and take a little more time and effort, it will be worthwhile as you find clarity and peace. Whether you are at a crossroads, debating what to do next, or unhappy and aware that something is missing, you will need to apply more effort and connect with God to discover your purpose in life.

The *Restored Discernment Companion Journal* is also a valuable tool for your small group, so you can readily discuss and share one another's responses to the questions. Whether you are at a crossroads and don't know what to do next or you are unhappy and feel like something is missing, you will need to put in more effort to find your life's purpose.

I pray that you will discover why you are stuck and experience a stunning life-changing breakthrough, allowing you to become the extraordinary person God had already created you to be!

A DISCERNMENT
COMPANION JOURNAL

Chapter One

DESPERATION

To identify why we can't move forward, it is important to take some time to analyze our thoughts. What is it you are thinking about yourself that has you paralyzed? Here is an exercise to help you identify these crippling thought processes that keep you from a breakthrough.

- Think about any disappointments or situations that made you feel bad or upset. Any event, regardless of size, could qualify. Name the event.

_____

_____

_____

_____

_____

- As best as you can, describe the feeling. Name how you feel.

_____

_____

_____

_____

_____

- Next, ask Jesus to take away the emotion.
- Next, ask Jesus to heal the wound the experience has left in your soul.

- Lastly, acknowledge Jesus' healing and thank Him for everything.
- Consider the same incident once more. Identify it and repeat the process if anything else emerges.
- Consider the event again, or wait a while, concentrate on anything else, and then consider the possibility again. There should be no sadness or negative feelings.

QUESTIONS

1. Define the areas in your life you feel stuck.

2. Which thought processes are you naturally drawn to when looking at situations or problems in your life? (e.g., Is your glass half-empty or half-full?)

3. What do you want? (Keep asking this question until it's refined!)

DISCERNING GOD'S VOICE

Read Jeremiah 29:10-14

"For this is what the LORD says: 'When seventy years have been completed for Babylon, I will visit you and fulfill My good word to you, to bring you back to this place. For I know the plans that I have for you,' declares the LORD, 'plans for prosperity and not for disaster, to give you a future and a hope. Then you will call upon Me and come and pray to Me, and I will listen to you. And you will seek Me and find *Me* when you search for Me with all your heart. I will let Myself be found by you,' declares the LORD, 'and I will restore your fortunes and gather you from all the nations and all the places where I have driven you,' declares the LORD, 'and I will bring you back to the place from where I sent you into exile.'

What words tend to stand out to you as you read these verses?

_____

_____

_____

Why do you think these words stand out?

_____

_____

_____

What do these verses reveal about God?

_____

_____

_____

How does God want me to respond as a result of reading these Scripture verses?

_____

_____

_____

Chapter Two

WHO AM I?

Take some time to sit in silence and read over yourself the verses from Song of Solomon 4:1, 7.

> "Behold, you are beautiful, my love, behold, you are beautiful!... you are altogether beautiful, my love; there is no flaw in you"

Write down anything thoughts that come to you as you pray about these verses.

_____

_____

_____

_____

QUESTIONS:

1.   What do you see when you look in the mirror?

_____

_____

_____

2. Aside from your appearance, what do you think about yourself?

_____

_____

_____

_____

_____

3. How do you think your thoughts affect the decisions you make?

_____

_____

_____

_____

4. Is it easy for you to receive compliments? Why or why not?

_____

_____

_____

_____

DISCERNING GOD'S VOICE

"Now may the God of peace, who brought up from the dead the great
Shepherd of the sheep through the blood of the eternal covenant, *that is,*
Jesus our Lord, equip you in every good thing to do His will, working in us
that which is pleasing in His sight, through Jesus Christ, to whom *be* the
glory forever and ever. Amen."
— Hebrews 13:20-21

What words tend to stand out to you as you read these verses?

Why do you think these words stand out?

What do these verses reveal about God?

How does God want me to respond as a result of reading these Scripture verses?

Chapter Three

TAKING THE NEXT
RIGHT STEP

Take a mini-retreat by finding a quiet spot to pray and read Philippians 2. Grab a drink, a pen and paper, or a journal to write things down. Begin by asking yourself the following questions and take them to the Lord.

Why am I stuck?

_____

_____

_____

What does God want of me?

_____

_____

_____

Why am I unhappy or dissatisfied?

_____

_____

_____

Where do you want me to go?

_____

_____

_____

_____

Ask God to give you clarity and courage with whatever He reveals. Read
Philippians 2. Did anything stand out to you? Please write it down. Then reread
Philippians 2, and write down anything else. Read again and write down anything
that has come to your mind. You are on your way to finding out your next right
step.

_____

_____

_____

_____

_____

_____

_____

_____

_____

QUESTIONS:

1. Are there some things you do that come naturally? List them below.

2. Have you ever noticed the joy that comes after doing something you know God had called you to do? Explain.

3. What holds you back from using the gifts you have been given?

DISCERNING GOD'S VOICE

"So then, my beloved, obedient as you have always been, not only when I am present but all the more now when I am absent, work out your salvation with fear and trembling. For God is the one who, for his good purpose, works in you both to desire and to work."
— Philippians 2:12-13

What words tend to stand out to you as you read these verses?

_____

_____

_____

Why do you think these words stand out?

_____

_____

_____

What do these verses reveal about God?

_____

_____

_____

How does God want me to respond as a result of reading these Scripture verses?

_____

_____

_____

Chapter Four

BRINGING OTHERS WITH YOU

QUESTIONS:

1.   Do you have a relatable community of people who encourage you? List them here.

---

2.   What prevents you from seeking a community to connect with?

---

3.   How can you reconnect or restore relationships in your life?

DISCERNING GOD'S VOICE

"Many plans are in a person's heart,
But the advice of the LORD will stand."
— Proverbs 19:21

What words tend to stand out to you as you read these verses?

_____

_____

_____

Why do you think these words stand out?

_____

_____

_____

_____

What do these verses reveal about God?

_____

_____

_____

_____

How does God want me to respond as a result of reading these Scripture verses?

_____

_____

_____

_____

Chapter Five

OBEDIENCE

QUESTIONS:

1. How do you feel about the word obedience? Explain why.

2. Is it easy for you to let go of your plans and compromise?

3. Why do you think we need to obey God's calling?

DISCERNING GOD'S VOICE

"As they were passing by in the morning, they saw the fig tree withered from the roots *up*. And being reminded, Peter said to Him, "Rabbi, look, the fig tree that You cursed has withered." And Jesus answered and said to them, "Have faith in God. Truly I say to you, whoever says to this mountain, 'Be taken up and thrown into the sea,' and does not doubt in his heart, but believes that what he says is going to happen, it will be *granted* to him. Therefore, I say to you, all things for which you pray and ask, believe that you have received them, and they will be *granted* to you."
— Mark 11:20:24

What words tend to stand out to you as you read these verses?

_____

_____

_____

Why do you think these words stand out?

_____

_____

_____

_____

What do these verses reveal about God?

_____

_____

_____

_____

_____

How does God want me to respond as a result of reading these Scripture verses?

_____

_____

_____

Chapter Six

YOUR SPIRITUAL LIFE

QUESTIONS:

1. Where are you at in your spiritual journey?

2. Where are you at in your spiritual journey?

3. How does your belief system affect you and your breakthrough?

DISCERNING GOD'S VOICE

"I will give You thanks with all my heart;
I will sing Your praises before the gods.
I will bow down toward Your holy temple
And give thanks to Your name for Your mercy and Your truth;
For You have made Your word great according to all Your name.
On the day I called, You answered me;
You made me bold *with* strength in my soul."

— Psalm 138:1-3

What words tend to stand out to you as you read these verses?

_____

_____

_____

_____

Why do you think these words stand out?

_____

_____

_____

_____

_____

What do these verses reveal about God?

_____

_____

_____

How does God want me to respond as a result of reading these Scripture verses?

_____

_____

_____

_____

Chapter Seven

YOU ARE AN OVERCOMER

QUESTIONS:

1.   How do you hold yourself back from moving forward?

2.   Is it easy to surrender all your cares and worries to God? Why or why not?

3.   How do you find joy in the waiting?

DISCERNING GOD'S VOICE

"Make me know Your ways, LORD;
Teach me Your paths.
Lead me in Your truth and teach me,
For You are the God of my salvation;
For You I wait all the day."
—Psalm 25:4-5

What words tend to stand out to you as you read these verses?

_____

_____

_____

Why do you think these words stand out?

_____

_____

_____

What do these verses reveal about God?

_____

_____

_____

How does God want me to respond as a result of reading these Scripture verses?

Chapter Eight

GOD'S PROMISE OF RESTORATION

QUESTIONS:

1. How do you view your life's challenges?

_____

_____

2. Which character from Scripture could you relate to in this chapter? Why?

_____

_____

_____

3. How might having faith that God will answer your prayers and provide help benefit you while you wait?

_____

_____

_____

DISCERNING GOD'S VOICE

"Therefore, I urge you, brothers *and sisters*, by the mercies of God, to present your bodies as a living and holy sacrifice, acceptable to God, *which is* your spiritual service of worship. And do not be conformed to this world, but be transformed by the renewing of your mind, so that you may prove what the will of God is, that which is good and acceptable and perfect."

—Romans 12:1-2

What words tend to stand out to you as you read these verses?

_____

_____

_____

Why do you think these words stand out?

_____

_____

_____

_____

What do these verses reveal about God?

_____

_____

_____

_____

How does God want me to respond as a result of reading these Scripture verses?

_____

_____

_____

_____

About the Author

Lisa Fahey is an author and speaker with over 20 years of experience of working with youth, adults and women in the church. She is the author of Rise Up, Women of God, A Scripture Study on 1 John and 2 John; Simply, A Women's Study on Ecclesiastes; Simply Advent; and Just As You Are, How Your Testimony Can Impact People In Ways You Never Thought Possible. All are meant to inspire, encourage and empower readers in their journey with God. Lisa draws on real-life stories and moments with God to inspire and encourage others.

At the age of 21, Lisa lost her first husband, which forever changed her approach to God and His word. Through her work, she shares how God helped her to grow and rise up as a woman of God, even during the trials of life.

Although "life is hard and messy," Lisa can show her readers through her Bible studies and books that the key to experiencing life completely is to follow their calling by serving God.

If this book has blessed you, please share the message with others by posting on social media using #restoredtoextraordinary

Website
www.lisafahey.com

Podcast
Lisa Fahey Ministry (Apple & Spotify)

Follow your Call Coaching
www.lisafahey.com/follow-your-call-coaching

Facebook
Christian Professional Women On Purpose - Lisa Fahey Ministry

Instagram lisafaheyministry

OTHER TITLES BY LISA FAHEY

SIMPLY: A WOMEN'S BIBLE STUDY ON ECCLESIASTES

A six week study of Ecclesiastes. This book of wisdom teaches us that living simply is the secret to experiencing life to the fullest.

RISE UP, WOMEN OF GOD: A STUDY OF 1 JOHN & 2 JOHN

This six week study of 1 and 2 John are the ideal Epistles to guide us through life's questions and confusing times.

SIMPLY ADVENT: A DAILY DEVOTIONAL TO PREPARE THE WAY FOR JESUS

Advent helps us simplify the chaos by preparing our hearts for Christmas.

JUST AS YOU ARE: HOW YOUR TESTIMONY CAN IMPACT PEOPLE IN WAYS YOU NEVER THOUGHT POSSIBLE

Your testimony can reach people for Christ in ways you never thought possible.

Made in the USA
Las Vegas, NV
19 September 2023

77839426R00031